RELA
CONTENTED?
HAPPY??

...then you must be missing something! Cartoonist Nick Miller explains why you should give up your carefree easy-going 21st century lifestyle and start to **TAKE LIFE SERIOUSLY!**

Would it help if those tiny labels they put on apples were apple flavoured?

Is it too late to watch
that documentary I missed
about asteroids?

If the Moon is supposed
to be made of cheese,
what are asteroids made of?

Should they have turned
Mike Tyson's autobiography
into a pop-up book?

Should I do something
about those rats
in the basement?

Did I spend too long
in the bath?

Should I have made
that blasphemous remark?

Should I tell NASA
one of their rovers
went a little off-course?

Is there any way to
check if my house is on
an animal migration route?

Should I stop scratching
the boil on my neck?

How many times
do I have to recycle
a boomerang?

Why do I never notice
paint marks until they're
too dry to get off?

Why is it that every full moon,
my shoes feel too tight?

Should I have kept
that doctor's appointment?

Isn't there supposed to be some sort of doll involved in a voodoo curse?

Could BT have been telling the truth when they blamed my connection problems on a voodoo curse?

Is it time to de-claw
the cat?

Should the cat be
tipping me?

Is there any point in
getting into a staring
contest with a
security camera?

Should I buy a new
pair of shoes or wait for
these 70's cubans
to wear through?

What is that smell..?

If hair, fingernails and
teeth all keep growing
after you die, how can
you tell when you're dead?

What happens if I get my toothpaste mixed up with my erection cream?

Is this chair evolving?

Should I start researching
my family history?

Should I have read
that Feng Shui guide
more carefully?

Should I have
fired the butler?

Why do I sometimes
feel like I live too near
France?

Have I really saved if
my utility company is only
taking an arm this time?

Is my hair too long,
or not long enough?

What happens if I use
hand cream on my face?

Should I have checked
the safety was on
before stashing that gun
under my seat?

Should I believe everything
I read in my horoscope?

Will my new ID card
reveal that I'm
actually from Mars?

If my ID card is stolen,
how am I supposed to know
who I am?

Why don't they move January
to the middle of the year,
when it's warmer?

Why didn't I know about
the extra setting
on this Lay-z-boy?

Am I becoming
less popular?

Is my mirror image
right-handed or left-handed?

Do cheaper roaming charges
mean I can finally afford
to phone my Polish plumber?

If I get clamped in an NHS car park, is there a six-month waiting list to have it taken off?

Should I have been
keeping up with the news?

Why are my texts
from Obama always
interrupted by
tweets from the Pope?

Why did the cat just
suddenly run away?

Why can I feel
a sudden draught?

Am I allergic to oxygen?

Do postal strikes explain
why half the letters I get
are in ancient Sumerian?

Why won't the garage
believe my car just
turned back into
a pumpkin?

Aren't unexplained phenomena supposed to happen *outdoors?*

Did I forget to pay
my reality bill?

Why does typing
"Paris Hilton" into Google
automatically switch
off safe search?

Should I be encouraging
the cat's hobbies?

Was it a good idea to try
Shroedinger's experiment
at home?

Is the IPCC being
optimistic about
sea level rises?

Is it time to mow
the seagrass carpet?

Was it a good idea
to buy a chair with
a "sell by" date?

Is "reverse smoking"
the best way to beat
the public smoking ban?

Am I worrying too much
about *Smurfs* sequels?

Should I see a doctor about
these fits of sneezing?

Did I leave my
spam filter off again?

Is it Spring already?

Is there such a thing
as a *straight* icon?

Is there enough
stress in my life?

Where are all the X's
and O's supposed to go
in this sudoku?

Is the ability to keep track of the plotlines in all these superhero movies itself a superpower?

Do houseflies actually
live in little houses?

If people were covered
in fur, would we spend less
on cosmetics, or more on
hairball cures?

Should I wait for the smoke alarm to go off or just act on my own initiative?

Have I been watching
too many cartoons?

Is it possible "wash and go" doesn't mean what I thought it meant?

Am I spending too much
time web surfing since
I discovered my laptop's
'vibrate' function?

Why can I hear the theme from *Mission Impossible*?

Was my choice of a nudist
holiday influenced by
Ryanair's luggage surcharges?

Should the new rules
for phone-in quizzes
include a reminder that
I've zero chance of winning?

Is my relationship
with the poltergeist
getting too complicated?

What's the medical term
for the area just below
the right elbow?

Have I been reading
to many manga?

Should the knowledge that
remote-control drones
are piloted by Americans
make me feel any safer?

Is it correct to use a
fish knife and fish fork
to eat tinned tuna?

Why do I miss the days
when user guides were
only sixty pages long?

Is it five o'clock
already?

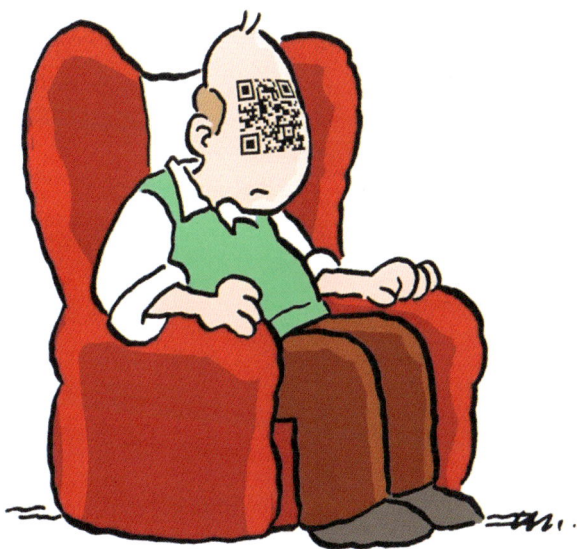

Are my bank's online
security measures
getting a bit much?

Should I worry about
some of the things
the cat brings in?

Is it time I stopped
talking to my houseplants?

Should I have checked the
pockets before I bought
this suit from Oxfam?

In an alternate universe,
am I having a party right now?

How come whenever
I write up my diary, I want
to skip to the last page to
see how things worked out?

Should I report these
Mafia drive-bys?

When I want to use a post
office, why do I have
to phone ahead to check
that it hasn't been closed?

Isn't "the elephant in the room" supposed to be a metaphor?

Why can't I remember
whether or not
I've got a goldfish?

Am I living too close
to the sea?

Was it a good idea to tell the police about next door's funny-smelling plants?

Should I see a doctor
about this, or just
apply to join the X Men?

Am I eating
too much wool?

Did I just stir my tea
clockwise or anti-clockwise?

Should I have got into
an argument with that
taxi driver?

Should I go on
holding in my sneezes?

Is it worth performing surgery at home just to avoid NHS phone charges?

Why do I keep buying
free range eggs?

Do gondoliers gondle?

Printed in Great Britain
by Amazon